South W...
FRAME *by* FRAME

CW00531553

Welcome to South Wales: Frame by Frame which tells in pictures the fascinating story of our region.

In the ensuing pages we get to see how important the coal trade was to Cardiff and the Valleys.

We pay a brief visit to Europe's youngest capital city and visit Barry Island, Porthcawl and other seaside resorts where thousands of holidaymakers have visited over the years.

We meet some of South Wales's greatest sporting heroes like Jim Driscoll and Jimmy Wilde, who was known as 'The Ghost with a Hammer in his Hand' and 'The Mighty Atom'.

The rugby icons featured include the legendary Gareth Edwards, the Cardiff scrum-half who played in 53 consecutive matches for Wales, and Newport's Ken Jones, who as well as being an outstanding rugby player was also an Olympic athlete.

We also take a sad look back at some of the coal mining disasters that have happened, like the one that took place in 1913 at the Universal, Senghenydd pit where some 439 miners died. And who could forget the Aberfan tip slide in 1966 which cost 144 lives? We also take a trip back in time when Hitler decided to drop his bombs on Cardiff, Newport, Swansea and other areas of South Wales.

On a lighter note, we will get to see some of our most famous showbiz personalities such as the fabulous Shirley Bassey and Tessie O'Shea. Also featured in this unique publication are Wales's top two football teams, Cardiff and Swansea, who this season will be playing each other in the Premier League. Expect the sparks to fly!

Heritage Editor: Harri Aston
Written by: Brian Lee
Designer: Ben Renshaw

Part of the Lost Britain **Collection**
© 2013 Trinity Mirror. All Rights Reserved

Managing Director: Ken Rogers
Senior Editor: Steve Hanrahan
Senior Art Editor: Rick Cooke
Editor: Paul Dove
Senior Marketing Executive: Claire Brown
Photosales: 0845 300 3021
Images: Mirrorpix, PA Photos
Printed by: William Gibbons

Horror of war De Burgh Street, Riverside, Cardiff, showing the destruction caused following a German air raid on January 2, 1941

Terror delivered from skies above

South Wales' industries and ports were targets of the German Luftwaffe in the Second World War but it was the civilian population that suffered the effects

Cardiff suffered its first wartime casualties when a single German plane bombed the ship San Felipe, in Cardiff Docks, killing seven men who were working in its holds on April 9, 1940.

Just 24 hours later, Swansea had its first casualties when the docks were targeted, resulting in 11 dockers being killed and about 30 seriously injured.

Barry had its first fatal air-raid on April 30, 1941, when four adults and one child were killed. While the west Wales resort of Tenby was bombed on October 21, 1941, when a lone bomber dropped four bombs on the town, killing a 76 year-old lady and injuring 15 other people.

Newport's darkest hour came on July 1, 1941, when a number of parachute mines were dropped on the area, killing 37 people.

On August 19, 1940, a Nazi bomber caused an inferno at Pembroke Docks when targeting oil tanks and started one of the biggest fires ever seen in Wales.

Five firefighters who rushed from Cardiff to deal with the blaze were killed and more than 260 firemen, some from as far as Bristol and Birmingham, were injured.

Cardiff's worst bombing raid, however, came in the early hours of the morning on January 2, 1941 when 115 tonnes of high explosives were dropped on the city.

When the all-clear siren was sounded in the early hours of the next morning it was discovered that 95 houses had been destroyed and a further 233 so badly damaged that they had to be knocked down. A total of 165 Cardiffians were killed and 168 had serious injuries.

▲ *Shocking damage* The damage caused by German bombers during air raids over Cardiff. This picture shows Albany Road, Cardiff, in January 1941

◀ **Only wreckage remains**
Swansea as dawn breaks after a three-night onslaught by the German Luftwaffe in February 1941

▲ **Ghost town**
Bomb damage in Swansea during the Second World War

▶ **Tanks a lot**
Children get a close-up view of one of the tanks outside Cardiff City Hall in September 1941

Housing problems *Damage in Glamorgan Street, Canton, Cardiff, following a German air raid. The raid, on January 2, 1941, killed 165 and left 328 homes either destroyed or in need of demolition. Another 426 houses were left uninhabitable until repaired*

Shocked onlookers *The damage caused following a raid on Partridge Road, Roath, in 1941*

▲ **Stadium damaged** *The damage caused to the stand at the Grangetown End of Cardiff Arms Park following a German air raid in 1941*

Winners' party *Victory in Europe Day celebrations, Edward Street in Cardiff, May 8, 1945*

▲ **Historic buildings, historic times** *Castle Bailey Street in Swansea, April 1940. A bailey sticking out amongst roof tops is all that remains of Swansea Castle. Underground dungeons have been converted into air-raid shelters. The old clock on the tower had been stopped for more than 200 years*

Bombed out *Shoe shop AG Meek on Albany Road, Roath, Cardiff revealing its bomb damage in the 1940s*

Great views Members of the Pendyrus Male Choir pose on the mountainside above Tylorstown and Ferndale in the Rhondda Fach on July 26, 1977

Highs and lows of life in the Valleys

The coal mines may have come and gone but friendliness, determination, courage and pride are all in abundance in the close-knit communities of South Wales

Cardiff, the capital city of Wales, owes its rise to the fact that it worked hand-in-hand with the coal trade of Wales and thus the Valleys which provided it.

The industrialisation of this mountainous area came about in the 18th century with the iron industry, and later when the coal fields were developed.

The iron and coal trade changed the landscape and what had once been a lightly inhabited area of Wales became more populated as immigrants looking for work were drawn to the Valleys.

Merthyr Tydfil was once Wales's largest town owing to the iron works at Cyfarthia and Dowlais and while at first coal was conveyed to Cardiff from the outlying districts on the back of mules, demand and supply meant that other methods such as railways and canals were built to transport these once precious materials.

However, nothing lasts for ever and with the demand for coal falling as oil superseded it as the fuel of choice in most industries, the death-knell for the industrialised era of the Valleys was sounded. One place that is dedicated to the preservation of this great Welsh heritage of the Valleys is the National Museum of Wales's Big Pit Industrial Heritage Museum at Blaenavon, which was a working coal mine from 1860-1980.

And as Mark Lawson-Jones, writing in The Little Book Of Wales, puts it: "Iron and coal changed Wales. Visit any former mining area and you will see how the landscape has been transformed. Close-knit communities with shared values and concerns mark out the Welsh Valleys as different. Friendliness and determination, courage and pride, are all in abundance.

"These characteristics have been roughly hewn from hundreds of years of not merely surviving, but flourishing, as a people. Facing the challenges together."

▲ *A river runs through it The Rhondda Fach running past the houses at Taff Street, Ferndale, on January 13, 1970*

On the move Parents watch over their children in Mary Ann Street, Dolwais, in 1973 on one of the streets earmarked for demolition

Perfect dress sense Mair Davies-Harrington, of Bargoed, was dressed up for St David's Day in 1960

Hilly streets A view of the streets of Mountain Ash, captured in 1988

▶ **Changes on the way** *This is Station Street, in Porth, as it was in 1900*

▼ **Old style transport** *Two trams at the terminus in Merthyr town centre, about 1930*

▲ **From on high** *Aerial shot of Merthyr town centre on August 9, 1989*

◀ **Not quite mod cons** *When residents of Glamorgan Terrace, at Tonypandy, felt a need to take a trip to the "Ty Bach", the name they gave to their toilet, they had to walk through their front door, cross the street and enter a small brick building. But like many such toilets in the Valleys, many were by this time used for storage, with new extensions built at the rear of their houses. This picture was snapped on January 27, 1978*

Braving the rain *Shoppers in Hannah Street, Porth, on October 24, 1964*

Busy street *Bargoed's High Street on September 19, 1962*

Quiet spot *Former miner Chris Price is photographed on a hillside near Mountain Ash in 1972*

Big pit *A photograph taken in 1984, of Blaenavon's former pit which is now a museum*

Balancing act George Pettican, with the aid of stilts, cleans the windows on the front of his shop in Ebbw Vale in March 1974

▲ **Community spirit** *Ferndale High Street crowded with people after a public meeting at a workingmen's club. It is not known when this photograph was taken*

Shopping street Shops in Adare Street, Bridgend, pictured on May 8, 1964

End of the line The closure of Britannia Colliery, near Bargoed, in December 1983 was an emotional day for Mervyn Thomas, left, of Aberbargoed, who had been at Britannia for seven years, and Wayne Rowlands, of Tir-y-Berth, who had been at Britannia for six years

Coal-fired pride in toughest of jobs

Mining was synonymous with South Wales, it was the industry that gave the life-blood to the local economy and employed thousands of hard-working men

The Western Mail, the national daily newspaper of Wales, back in 1925 published a book by Elizabeth Phillips called Pioneers Of The Welsh Coalfield, which claimed coal was being worked in Felin Fach, Llanfabon, as long ago as 1283.

One thing we know for certain is that Cardiff, by the late 1890s, was the biggest coal exporter in the world. On the eve of the First World War, coal exports reached a peak of 13 million tonnes.

However, this search for the 'black diamond' came at a huge price.

The first recorded big disaster was when 59 men died at the Cwmllynfell Colliery in 1825.

Over the years, hundreds of miners have been killed in individual accidents but just some of the other major disasters include the ones at Cymmer Old Pit in 1856 when 114 miners died, 1860 when 142 miners lost their lives at Risca Black Vein, and in 1878 when 268 people lost their lives at the Prince of Wales Colliery at Abercarn.

It was 100 years ago this year, on October 14, 1913, that the biggest coal mining disaster took place at the Universal, Senghenydd, coal mine when 439 miners were killed.

Mention must also be made of the Aberfan tip-slide that killed 144 people including 116 children on October 21, 1966.

The decline of the coal and iron industries during the 1960s and 1970s sounded the death-knell for Cardiff's docklands and by the late 1980s the area had become a scene of dereliction and wasteland.

It was in 1995 that Cardiff presented the Freedom of the City to the South Wales miners for their toil and sacrifice. A memorial plaque at Mardy Colliery, unveiled on December 21, 1990, really says it all: "This memorial commemorates the closure of Mardy Colliery. The last of 53 major collieries in the 150-year history of coal mining in the Rhondda valleys. A permanent reminder of the tragedies and sorrow endured and a tribute to the mighty courage, heroism and pride of the Rhondda miner and his family. A glorious past is surely the cornerstone of a glorious future."

▲ *Showbiz guest* Drag artist Danny La Rue, centre, swapped his ladies' wig for a mining helmet and visited Oakdale Colliery, near Blackwood in 1975. Danny, pictured in the pit-cage, had to put up with pit humour but signed autographs by lamplight and resurfaced with a piece of coal

Festive treat Father Christmas arrives at Big Pit, Blaenavon, on December 4, 1986 where he was in his grotto underground each weekend until Christmas

Still surviving A coal miner checks his lamp at a South Wales colliery, pictured on April 19, 1990

▲ **The way it was** Penallta Colliery at Hengoed, pictured on June 23, 1970

▲ **Hard work** The coal is dredged in buckets from the bed of Sirhowy at Pontllanfraith, near Blackwood, in September 1947. The coal, still wet, is loaded on to the waiting lorry and transported

Tough times Betws Colliery manager Vince Rogers in August 1984

Proud men *Miners who came up from underground for the last time at Britannia Colliery, near Bargoed, which closed in December 1983. Most were transferred to other pits, while some took redundancy*

▶ **Bitter fight**
Welsh miners on strike drew their last full week's pay at Nine Mile Point Colliery in Monmouthshire in March 1944

▲ **Colliery closure** *Britannia Colliery, near Bargoed, on the eve of its closure*

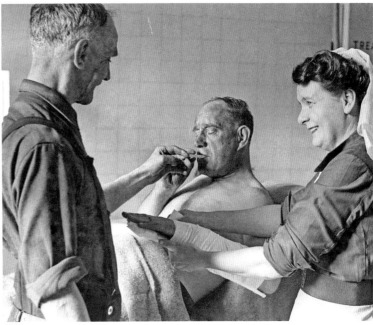

▲ **Have a smoke** An injured miner enjoys a cigarette while being tended to in the Coegnant Colliery medical centre in February 1949

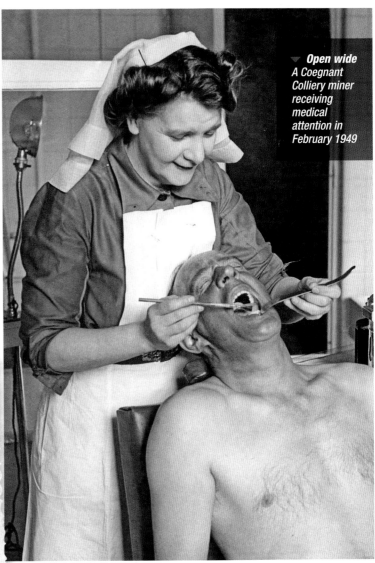

▼ **Open wide** A Coegnant Colliery miner receiving medical attention in February 1949

◄ **Wash time** A miner at the Windsor Colliery, Abertridwr, enjoys a shave with one of the electric razors installed at the colliery. His two grimy 'butties' watch with interest, September 1952

Pain and grief *A visibly upset Queen and Prince Philip visiting Aberfan and talking to parents in October 1966*

▲ Shocking aftermath *Rescuers stare at the remains of a Ford saloon car following the landslide in Aberfan*

◀ History of disaster *The Universal Colliery disaster in 1913 in which 439 men were killed at Senghenydd*

Moment of horror Workers desperately try to clear debris following the landslide in Aberfan in October 1966

▲ **Search goes on** Rescue workers continue the search under floodlights at some of the houses engulfed by the slag heap in Aberfan in 1966

Royal visitor The Duke of Edinburgh as he surveys the devastating scene in Aberfan

▶ **Seafront scene** *A photograph of Penarth's pier and Esplanade taken in April 1950*

Happy days beside the Welsh seaside

Blessed with some of the most beautiful coastline in the whole of the British Isles, generations have spent many a happy time enjoying our superb beaches

Visits to the seaside in South Wales meant trips to Barry Island, Porthcawl Lavernock and Penarth. Favourite with most children was Barry Island with its popular Figure 8 Railway and Pat Collins's showground, now long-gone like the Scenic Railway which replaced the Figure 8 Railway in 1939.

Who can forget Dorothy Arcade with its What The Butler Saw and many other penny attractions such as The Laughing Policeman?

Today, Barry Island is probably best known for its Gavin and Stacey tour made famous by the popular television series.

It is still a great place for a traditional family holiday though, with its beautiful sandy beach, candy floss, ice-cream, fish and chips and Kiss Me Quick hats!

For those who fancy a quieter time, there is the nearby Jackson Bay with its coastal walks and sea views. Also close by is Cold Knap, which once boasted a big open-air swimming pool. It is also a good place to go fishing and wind surfing.

When coal was king, miners and their families would flock to the caravan park in Trecco Bay, Porthcawl, for their annual fortnight's holiday.

Ideal for building sand castles, sunbathing and swimming, not to mention donkey rides, was nearby Sandy Bay which is also close to the town centre.

However, Porthcawl's hidden jewel is the remote and historical Sker Beach which backs on to the Kenfig National Park Reserve and has wonderful views of the Gower and Swansea.

It was from Lavernock Point, near Penarth, that Marconi received the first radio transmission across the sea in 1897.

Penarth is famous for its new pavilion and pier, where in the 1950s and 60s hundreds of youngsters would go dancing in the old Marina Ballroom. Constructed in 1894 and spanning 219 yards in length it is a good place to go fishing and many fishing contests take place along both sides of the pier.

▲ *Ride away*
Children enjoy that age-old pleasure of the beach, the traditional donkey ride

▶ **All aboard**
The mammoth
queue in Tenby
for the Caldey
Island trip during
the August bank
holiday of 1978

▼ **The old and
the new** Retired
miner John
James, aged
63, of Cwmbran,
still enjoyed the
traditional holiday
at Trecco Bay,
Porthcawl, on July
28, 1980

▲ **Crowds of people** All the fun of the fair for the Whitsun
holidaymakers at Barry Island on June 2, 1968

▲ **Happy days** Penarth in 1965

Up, up and away *A redcoat and a camper enjoy a ride in the Butlins rope railway high above the camp at Barry Island on June 13, 1967*

◀ **Swimming joy** *Holidaymakers enjoy the indoor swimming pool at Butlins on July 1, 1965*

▲ **Come dancing** *Anthony Latimer, left, and Verona Abbott are presented with the Butlins Sequence (Old Time) Under 35 Pre-Championship Trophy at Barry Island on September 27, 1979*

Ever popular Holidaymakers enjoy the sand and sunshine at Porthcawl on Bank Holiday Monday, May 28, 1990

Harbour view Boats tied to Tenby Harbour wall in the bright sun on June 10, 1960

▶ **Fabulous food** An old lady enjoying fish and chips during a day out to the beach at Trecco Bay, August 6, 1977

Standing room only Big crowds enjoy the sun at Barry Island in June 1949

▶ **Chips off the old block** Sun, sand and fish and chips at Trecco Bay, August 6, 1977

▶ **Natural wonder** People took advantage of the late afternoon sunshine to get a spot of sunbathing in the brilliant sunshine at Lavernock beach on this day in May 1965

▶ **Traffic control** A policeman controls the dangerous crossing point at Barry Island in June 1960

Future PM James Callaghan on holiday in August 1957 in St Davids, Pembrokeshire, with his wife and children Margaret (now Baroness Jay), Julia, Michael and dog Kim

◀ **Holiday destination** The caravan site at Fontygary with the village in the background in August 1986

Water laugh A moment of high excitement at Porthcawl with a ride on the water chute at Coney Beach Funfair on May 30, 1968

All quiet Mumbles Pier, pictured on July 9, 1956

▶ **Soaked** At the bottom of the water chute ride at Coney Beach Funfair, August 2, 1990

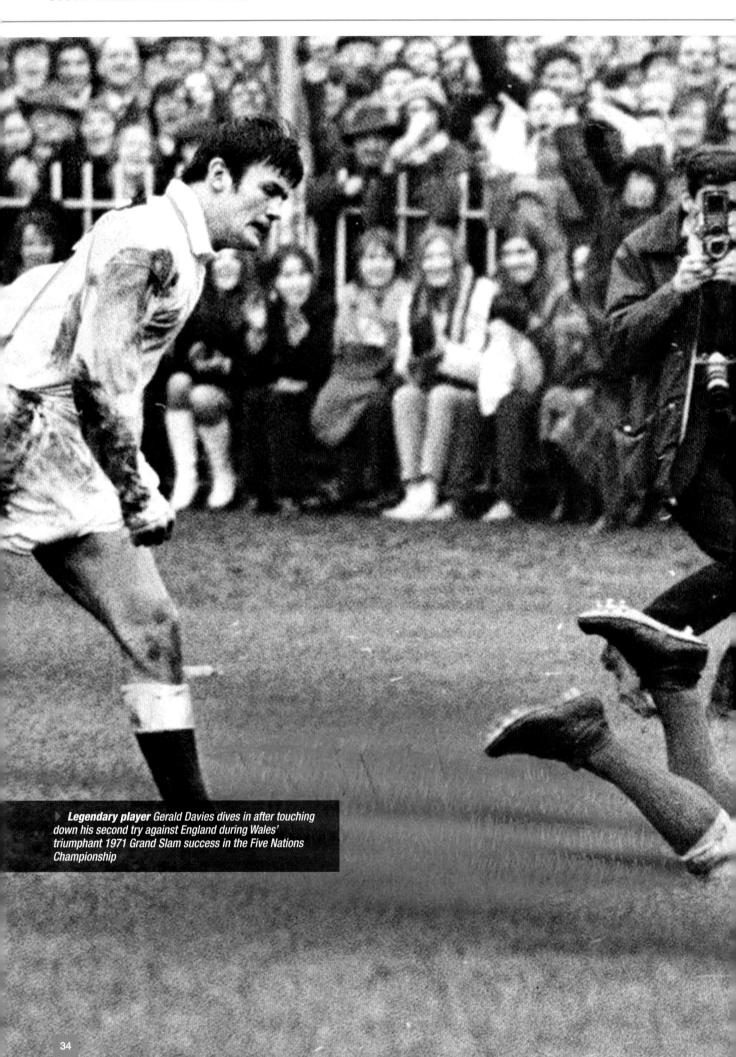

▶ **Legendary player** *Gerald Davies dives in after touching down his second try against England during Wales' triumphant 1971 Grand Slam success in the Five Nations Championship*

Stars who shined on the rugby field

It is Wales' national game and our greatest sporting heroes have emerged in dramatic fashion, playing some of the most sublime rugby ever seen

Some of the greatest players to have graced the game of rugby honed their skills on the playing fields of South Wales.

One of the first true stars of the game was Swansea full-back Billy Bancroft (1871-1959), who played 33 consecutive matches for Wales and was captain on 11 occasions. His brother, Jack (1879-1942), won eight caps.

Mervyn Davies, of Swansea, was regarded as the best number eight in the world, while Neath-born Phil Davies played for Wales 45 times between 1985-1995.

John Dawes, who played for Wales between 1964-1971, and who captained the Barbarians to a memorable win over New Zealand in 1973, was awarded an OBE.

An MBE went to the legendary Gareth Edwards, the Cardiff scrum-half who played in 53 consecutive internationals and captained his country at the tender age of 20 years and seven months.

Cardiff's Terry Holmes, who played for the Lions on their South Africa and New Zealand tours in 1980 and 1983 respectively, won a record number of youth caps and represented his country on 25 occasions.

Newport's Keith Jarrett made his international debut at just 18 and also played a couple of first-class cricket matches for Glamorgan in 1967 before playing rugby as a professional for Barrow in 1969. The Rhondda's Neil Jenkins is another Welsh rugby icon who scored 399 points for Wales and replaced Paul Thorburn as Wales's leading points scorer in the 1990s.

Another Welsh rugby icon who hailed from the Valleys was Cliff Jones, who was capped 13 times in the 1930s. He later became president of the Welsh Rugby Union and was awarded the OBE.

Olympic sprinter Ken Jones, of Newport, won 44 Welsh caps between 1947 and 1957 and another sprinter, JJ Williams who was born on April 1, 1948, was certainly no fool as he scored 12 tries for Wales in 30 consecutive games between 1973-79 and represented Wales at the 1970 Commonwealth Games in Edinburgh.

Cardiff's JPR Williams, who was previously the most capped Welsh rugby player with 55 appearances to his name, was also very good with the tennis racquet and won the Wimbledon junior singles title in 1966.

Bleddyn Williams, born in Taffs Well in 1923, is a legend in Welsh rugby circles. He captained the Lions five times and during the 1947/8 season he scored 41 tries in 31 matches for Cardiff, who went through that season undefeated.

These are just some of the South Walian rugby players who made a name for themselves in our national sport.

▲ **On the chase**
Bleddyn Williams is about to be tackled as he chases his own kick, as Wales are defeated by France 3-11 on February 21, 1948

▶ **Lion heart**
Bryn Meredith,
who was part
of the all-Welsh
front row that
played South
Africa on the 1955
Lions tour

▲ **Pacy winger** JJ Williams, the Llanelli and Wales star,
pictured in January 1974

▲ **Seventies
star** Mervyn
Davies being led
off the pitch with
a injury in an
encounter with
France in March
1972

▶ **The King**
Barry John, the
Welsh fly-half,
makes a break
against England
in March 1970

Murrayfield here we come
The Wales team and officials board the aircraft for their flight to Edinburgh on February 5, 1971. Pictured are rugby greats Derek Quinnell, Gareth Edwards, Barry John, Phil Bennett, John Dawes, Gerald Davies, John Taylor, and coach Clive Rowlands among others

▲ **Rugby icon** Cliff Jones, who was capped 13 times in the 1930s

▲ **Flowing move** Gareth Edwards throws out a pass and Phil Bennett is pictured in the background during the Barbarians' game against New Zealand in January 1973

◀ **Class act** Gareth Edwards proves too strong for Ireland's Mike Gibson as he crosses for his second try in the 23-9 Triple Crown win of 1971 at Cardiff Arms Park

Greatest game ever? John Dawes, the Barbarians captain, is carried from the field following his team's triumph against the All Blacks, January 27, 1973

▲ **Full flow** JPR Williams with the ball being supported by Gerald Davies on his left

◄ **Farewell game** Neil Jenkins runs with the ball during his last appearance in a Welsh shirt, against the Barbarians in 2003

◀ **Meeting of legends** Billy Bancroft, right, congratulates Ken Jones, who was poised to win a record-equalling 35th cap in a game against Scotland in 1954

▼ **All hail the heroes** Keith Jarrett playing for Wales against England in 1967

▼ **More glory** Phil Bennett in action for Wales at Murrayfield on March 19, 1977. Wales went on to win the match 18-9, retaining the Triple Crown

Merlin Ieuan Evans makes a break for Wales against Scotland in 1988

Yesterdays

Don't miss the great nostalgia packages in the South Wales Echo every week. On Tuesday, our Yesterdays Extra features Dan O'Neill, the Kairdiff Kid, remembering great moments in Cardiff's past; Tuesdays also features the 12-page Yesterdays pullout, packed with great pictures and memories from our archives; on Friday, columnist Brian Lee profiles great Cardiff characters and on Saturday our special double-page features highlight more memories, historic front pages and views of Cardiff then and now.

LOVE YOUR HISTORY?
LOVE WALES

Are you an expert on local history? Do you know the stories behind things like Cardiff's parks or the key role South Wales played in the Industrial Revolution? If you have knowledge of any specific heritage subject, please get in touch and help play an important part in Britain's biggest-ever media heritage project. With your support, we will be bringing history back to life...

E-mail the Heritage Editor:

harri.aston@trinitymirror.com

LOST WALES

A city that has seen big changes

From a sleepy coastal town to a major industrial giant and port, the 'Welsh Chicago' has undergone many incredible transformations

City landmark A photograph of Cardiff Castle taken around 1940

In 2005, there were celebrations in Cardiff to celebrate its 50th year as the capital city of Wales and 100 years as a city. And standing in the heart of it all is Cardiff's oldest building, the castle.

The other great feature of Cardiff is its civic centre which includes the most magnificent Edwardian buildings in the country.

First founded by the Roman legions nearly 2,000 years ago, Cardiff – once known as the 'Welsh Chicago' because of its rapid expansion – has always been a city of change and before the industrial revolution Cardiff was just a sleepy little town on the South Wales coast.

That was until mules started arriving laden with coal from the Welsh valleys. The Industrial Revolution took hold, the iron and coal trade took off and a vast complex of docks spread rapidly around the town's natural harbour. The Glamorgan Canal was built to transport the iron and coal, and the railways arrived. By the late 19th century Cardiff had become the largest coal-exporting port in the world.

But the decline in the coal and iron industries after the Second World War sounded the death-knell for Cardiff's docklands.

By the 1960s, Tiger Bay had become a scene of dereliction and, with a final sweep of the bulldozer, a whole way of life disappeared.

Hard to believe now that the area is home to the National Assembly of Wales, the Wales Millennium Centre, the Glamorgan County Offices, thousands of new apartments, cinemas, cafes, shops, commercial buildings, hotels, and much, much more, providing work and entertainment for thousands of Cardiffians and tourists.

▲ *Sixties vision*
An aerial shot of Cardiff, captured on May 15, 1965

▲ **Flipping magic** *Pancake Day in Cardiff in 1961 and a pancake race is organised in aid of Congo Relief at Berram Road, Roath. Pictured is the over-40s race*

▲ **Pride in the nation** *Children in this Cardiff school celebrate St David's Day by wearing national dress, March 1, 1944*

▶ **Busy port** *The old docks in Cardiff, October 23, 1962*

▲ *International flavour* Cardiff was the venue for an impressive Islamic procession, pictured on April 18, 1954, in which followers from many lands took part. The procession of members of the Zaoula Islamia Allauia Religious Society took place in Bute Street

▶ *Capital gain* The scene outside the City Hall when the announcement of the granting of capital status was read on December 20, 1955

National pride Festival of Wales, May 1958. The parade marches past the City Hall

◀ **Sporting excellence** Aerial shot of the area that was later demolished. Cardiff Arms Park is in the background, alongside the Glamorgan County Cricket Ground. The houses in the foreground were part of 'Temperance Town', photographed in the 1930s

Spiritual procession A Roman Catholic procession through the streets of Cardiff makes its way to the castle in June 1939

▲ **Swinging fun**
Four youngsters enjoying the summer sunshine at a play area in the Cardiff docks area in the mid-1970s

◀ **Poor housing**
Yvonne Evans of Bute Street, with her children, Janet, three, Stephen, two and Philip, three months, outside the condemned house in which she lived by the docks of Butetown in August 1969

▲ **Game time** The old iron drinking fountain at the entrance to Cardiff Docks was no longer working but it still attracted local youngsters who adapted it for one of their games in December 1969. Pictured are, from left, 14 year-old Akbar Hassin, 13 year old Peter Scott and seven-year-old Paul Santos

▲ **Victorian homes** September 20, 1962 and a young child sits in the gutter in Cycle Street with the abattoir, demolished in 1970, pictured on the left

Better future The future is all theirs. Stephen Powell of Smith Street, left, and his friend Eric Horne of Robinson Square, Splott, talk of their future, amid broken walls and the towering steelworks, as they are about to be re-housed in Tremorfa in May 1970

▸ **Famous result** Cardiff welcomed Real Madrid to Ninian Park on March 10, 1971, for the first leg of the Cup Winners' Cup quarter-final in which City's Brian Clarke scored the only goal. Playing in front of 47,000 people, Cardiff recorded one of the biggest victories in their history

The glory days of mighty Bluebirds

Cardiff City are back in the big time, hoping for a return to the days when they humbled one of the most glamorous names in world football and won the FA Cup at Wembley

IT was an image that will live long with any Cardiff City fan who was there to see it.

The final whistle sounded and an emotional Craig Bellamy crumpled to his knees.

The referee's blast had signalled the end of the Bluebirds' goalless draw with Charlton – and with it more than 50 years of waiting.

Bellamy and the rest of Malky Mackay's class of 2013 had secured their place in history after sealing promotion to the Premier League and bringing top-flight football back to the Welsh capital.

It had been an incredible journey, one that had seen the club go from blue to red under Malaysian businessman Vincent Tan, and which stretches far beyond Mackay's input.

Far beyond even the last time Cardiff dined at English football's top table at Ninian Park in the early 1960s.

Who could forget the Bluebirds' very own Roaring Twenties where an FA Cup final defeat in 1925 – one year after missing out on the league title on goal ratio – proved only to deny the club becoming the first to take a major prize out of England by two seasons. For it was at Wembley in 1927, on St George's Day of all days, where Fred Keenor's men sunk Arsenal to carry the FA Cup back over the Severn.

It was a success that Cardiff struggled to live up to at times, but top-level football in the 1950s was followed by the nearly men of the 1970s when a packed Ninian Park struck fear into teams from all over the continent, including the mighty Real Madrid.

Like every club, there were lows as well as highs, Cardiff spending too many years to remember in the lower leagues.

But the resurgence began at the start of the new millennium, local heroes emerging in the form of Robert Earnshaw.

There was the joy and despair of visits to Wembley where proud supporters marched on London for the FA Cup final, Carling Cup final and the Championship play-off final, only to witness defeats.

But the image of that night in April secured a new dawn – and promises to add to the Bluebirds' magical moments.

▲ **Heads up**
Cardiff City versus Hamburg and Cardiff's Norman Dean heads the ball over the head of Hans Schulz towards goal on May 1, 1968

▶ **Celebration** Youngsters run on to the pitch and mob Cardiff captain Brian Harris after he scores their second goal against Hamburg, however the Bluebirds lost the game 3-2 (4-3 on aggregate)

▶ **Exciting times** Cardiff City manager Jimmy Scoular and his players in the dressing room at Ninian Park looking at the South Wales Echo's Real Madrid special

▲ **Phenomenal scenes** Cardiff fans on the Bob Bank cheer as Norman Dean scores the team's first goal in front of 43,070 packed into Ninian Park for the Hamburg match, which the Bluebirds lost 3-2 (4-3 on aggregate)

▶ **Exalted visitors** Ninian Park under the floodlights was always a special place, especially if the opposition was Real Madrid

Final drama *Cardiff City captain Trevor Ford shakes hands with Swansea skipper Ivor Allchurch in front of referee Mervyn Griffiths before the Welsh Cup final on April 28, 1956, which the Bluebirds won 3-2*

▷ **Gentle giant** The legendary John Charles in his Cardiff City playing days, July 6, 1964

▲ **Star in the making** Sixteen-year-old John Toshack enjoys a celebration drink following his debut, coming on as substitute to score the final goal in a 3-1 win over Leyton Orient at Ninian Park in November 1965

◁ **Important figure** Lord Ninian Stuart (with cigarette) at the football match between Cardiff City and Swansea on November 23, 1908. Ninian Park was named after him after he agreed to be Cardiff City's guarantor for the new ground. Lord Ninian was killed in action during the First World War

COMMITTEE

▶ **Victorious team** The Cardiff City heroes who won the 1927 FA Cup, pictured on April 30, 1927. They are (back row, from left) George Latham (trainer), Jimmy Nelson, Tom Farquharson, Tom Watson, George McLachlan (middle row) Tom Sloan, Sam Irving, Fred Keenor (captain), Billy Hardy, Len Davies. (front row) Ernie Curtism and Hughie Ferguson

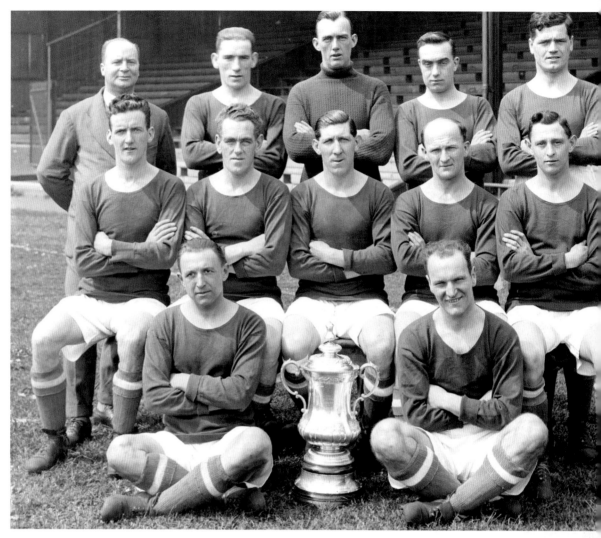

▶ **Final action** Cardiff City's Billy Hardy jumps highest to clear an Arsenal attack during the first half of the 1927 FA Cup final at Wembley

◄ **Historic moment** *Cardiff City's Len Davies celebrates after Hughie Ferguson's shot is fumbled by Arsenal goalkeeper Dan Lewis and ends up in the net*

▼ **Taste of success** *Cardiff City celebrating their cup success. They are, from left, Fred Keenor offering Billy Hardy a drink, from the FA Cup watched by City reserve Tom Pirie, holding the lid. In the background, manager Fred Stewart talks to Cardiff Lord Mayor William Gray*

On the spot Swansea's Willie Screen scores from a penalty against Aston Villa at the Vetch Field on August 29, 1970

Swans flying high after tough times

Few football clubs on the planet have witnessed the highs and lows that Swansea City have put their fans through – the club is a byword for a sporting roller-coaster ride

EVERY football club has their story. It just so happens that Swansea City's tale of triumphs and tribulations is greater than most.

Few clubs anywhere have seen the rises and falls enjoyed and endured by supporters of this proud club.

Indeed, the image of Ashley Williams and Garry Monk lifting the 2013 League Cup at Wembley for the club's first major English prize was a fitting moment to commemorate the club's centenary season.

For it was a success made all the more sweeter by what had gone on before it.

Because drama has never been far away from the football club born by the sea in 1912.

In the dark days of the mid-1970s, directors had to go pleading for votes for re-election to the Football League. A decade later, the latest-of-late High Court reprieves on a winding-up order allowed the gates of the ramshackle, yet romantic, Vetch Field to be re-opened.

The worries returned at the start of the millennium as bills went unpaid only for fans to light the way out of the Swans' darkest hour, taking control of the club they love.

And so, as the club waved goodbye to the Vetch in 2005 to set up modern base at the Liberty Stadium, a return to the glory days in the Premier League beckoned.

They had reached the top before, an early 1980s race to the First Division under John Toshack where the wonderful Welsh talents of Robbie James, Alan Curtis and Leighton James excelled.

In 2011, they did it again with the likes of Leon Britton playing in every division with a panache that won admirers throughout the country.

The style invoked the play of the 1950s where stars like Cliff Jones, Mel Charles and Ivor Allchurch dazzled in Swansea white.

And having had their fairy-tale runs in cups before, including trips to Wembley and giant-killing stories for the ages, a silver lining came in the form of silverware in that 5-0 romp over Bradford.

A club bought for £1, whose fans refused to die, etching their name into the history books. Swansea's story has to be seen to be believed.

▲ *International encounter* *Swansea Town versus Northern France Select at the Vetch Field on April 26, 1956. Swansea's Mel Charles, brother of John, aims for goal watched right by Ivor Allchurch*

Here we go Smiles all around at Preston North End after a 3-1 win on May 2, 1981 guaranteed a third promotion in four seasons and Swansea City joined the footballing elite. Player-manager John Toshack celebrates with his director and chairman Malcolm Struel, (dark glasses)

▲ **Famous goal** John Toshack heads Swansea City's winning goal against Chesterfield to seal promotion to Division Two at the Vetch Field in 1979

▲ **Top-flight heroes** Swansea City players enjoy a tour of the city on May 10, 1981 following their promotion to Division One

▶ **Action** A Leicester City player attempts to kick the ball off the line following a header from a Swansea player on April 14, 1965

▲ Classic encounter
Cardiff's Brian Walsh sends in a low drive which puts the visitors three goals up at the Vetch Field. Swansea fought back to draw the game 3-3. From left; Mel Nurse, Brian Walsh, Dixie Hale, Dai Thomas and John King, the Swansea goalkeeper, March 26, 1960

▶ Local rivals
The Swans' Brayley Reynolds beats the Cardiff keeper but his shot is cleared off the line during a game in February 1960

▲ **Going up!** Swansea players make a triumphant tour of the Vetch Field following their promotion to the First Division, May 5, 1981

▶ **Big Bob**
Swansea's former England international Bob Latchford climbs above the Norwich City defence to head goalward at the Vetch Field September 5, 1982

Going fourth
Swansea's Brian Evans scoring the Swans' first of four goals against Oldham goalkeeper Barry Gordine, February 8, 1970

All action Len Allchurch, brother of Ivor, in action for Swansea against Liverpool in 1958, with the Reds' Ronnie Moran in the background

▲ **Rising star** Dean Saunders heads in Swansea City's first goal against Brentford at the Vetch Field, February 10, 1985

◄ **What's in a name?** Swansea Town, as they were then, in home action against Arsenal on January 25, 1958

Promotion drive *Swans legend Robbie James (right) and a delighted Nigel Stephenson turn to celebrate Stevenson's goal against Blackburn Rovers at the Vetch Field on April 5, 1981*

▲ **Star striker** *Swansea player Brayley Reynolds takes a flying leap in January, 1963. After he retired from football Reynolds, worked at Penallta Colliery, near Hengoed*

Local boy *Leeds United legend Jack Charlton closes in on Swansea winger Kenny Morgans at the Vetch Field in September 1962. Morgans, born in Swansea, had played for Manchester United but suffered serious injuries in the Munich air crash in 1958 and his career never recovered. He was the youngest of the Busby Babes and the last survivor to be pulled from the wreckage of the plane, six hours after the crash*

Cup winners *Captain Ashley Williams, right, and his teammates celebrate winning the Capital One Cup which Swansea City won after beating Bradford City 5-0 at Wembley*

▶ **Penalty offence** *Bradford goalkeeper fouls Matt Duke, leading to his sending off and a penalty for Swansea*

We're going up *Swansea celebrate scoring a goal in the 2011 play-off final against Reading*

Star attraction Tom Jones entertains the crowds in Penarth on July 7, 1965, to raise money for the Cogan Crash Appeal Fund, set up to help two people who were badly injured when they were involved in a collision with a van. He performed at both the Paget Rooms and the Marina Ballroom on the same evening

Showbiz stars who entertain the world

Some of the 20th century's greatest icons of stage and screen have emerged from the wealth of talent in South Wales

When it comes to great showbiz stars they don't come any better than Cardiff's own Ivor Novello (1893-1951), a star of stage and screen who was dubbed 'The Valentino of England'.

He wrote many songs and musicals and the statue of him in Cardiff Bay is well deserved. Also from Cardiff came Tessie O'Shea (1914-1995), known as Two-Ton Tessie, who topped the bill at the London Palladium during the war and who many years later won a Tony award on Broadway.

Neath-born Ray Milland (1905-1986) won an Oscar for playing an alcoholic in the film The Lost Weekend in 1945 and Richard Burton (1925-1984) was nominated for an Academy award seven times without winning one.

Pontypridd singer Tom Jones, born in 1940, has enjoyed worldwide fame thanks to hits such as It's Not Unusual and Delilah. Caerphilly-born Tommy Cooper (1922-1984) is still recognised by many as Britain's best-loved comedian, while film actor Sir Anthony Hopkins won an Academy Award for The Silence Of The Lambs.

Swansea-born Catherine Zeta-Jones also won an Academy Award for Best Supporting Actress in the 2002 musical Chicago.

Dame Shirley Bassey, born in the Tiger Bay area of Cardiff in 1937, has been an international star for many years. She was awarded the Britannia Award in 1977 as the best female singer of the past 50 years.

Dorothy Squires (1915-1998), whose life story has recently been made into the play Say It With Flowers and who married film actor Roger Moore, trod the boards at the London Palladium, Carnegie Hall and the Albert Hall amongst other places.

Elvis Presley and Frank Sinatra were two of her greatest fans but sadly she died in poverty, spending the last days of her life in the home of one of her fans.

More recently, Cardiff's Charlotte Church became the youngest singer to have a number one album in the classical charts with her first album *Voice of an Angel* when she was just 12 years old. She has sold more than 10 million records worldwide and now writes her own songs.

Neath's Katherine Jenkins has a number of best selling albums to her name and her range of music includes pop songs, hymns and opera. While the Manic Street Preachers, formed in the Blackwood area of Gwent, have been one of Wales' most successful rock bands.

▲ *Royal fan*
Prince Charles meeting Dame Shirley Bassey at a charity show at Wembley in November 1979

▶ **Young face** Shirley Bassey in 1956

▶ **Singing hope** Welsh singer Mary Hopkin was chosen to represent Britain at the Eurovision Song Contest in 1970

▶ **Full costume** Actress Diana Rigg and Anthony Hopkins in an Old Vic Theatre production of Macbeth in 1972

▲ **Multi-talented** Ivor Novello, actor, singer and composer

On the right road Tom Jones shows his certificate after passing his driving test in Newport in March 1967

Ear, ear Comic magician Tommy Cooper on July 18, 1977

Music hall legend *Cardiff's Tessie O'Shea, known as Two-Ton Tessie, with her banjo in Llandaff in February 1983*

Singing star *Harry Secombe looks just right for his role as Schippel, a plumber with a golden tenor voice, in The Plumber's Progress, which had its first night at the Prince of Wales Theatre on October 8, 1975*

Natural talent *Tom Jones performing on TV on January 30, 1969*

Famous duo *Richard Burton and Elizabeth Taylor at the premiere of Around the World in 80 Days at the Coliseum in London in March 1968*

◀ **Lighting up** Richard Burton shooting The Spy Who Came In From The Cold in 1965

▶ **British film star** Hollywood star Ray Milland is reunited with the Flying Scotsman for its diamond jubilee in 1983. Milland, born in Neath, starred in the 1929 film The Flying Scotsman

▶ *Voice of an angel* Charlotte Church pictured in 1999 when she was 13

▲ *Stage star* Singer Dorothy Squires performing at Newcastle City Hall January 23 1971

Beloved pets Dorothy Squires with her pet dogs in September 1949

◀ *High note* Katherine Jenkins sings before the Wales v South Africa rugby game in 2005

▶ **The Mighty Atom** Jimmy Wilde fighting the American Memphis Pal Moore in London on July 18, 1919, winning in the 20th round on points

Nation punches above its weight

We have produced a range of individual heroes in all manner of sports, with the fight game being particularly well served by South Wales stars

Over the years, South Wales has produced a number of sporting greats, be they on the soccer or rugby field, in the boxing ring on the racecourse or in the swimming pool.

Cardiff swimmer Paulo Radmilovic (1886-1968) won gold medals at the Olympic Games of 1908, 1912 and 1920.

Tom Richards won the silver medal in the marathon at the London Olympic Games in 1948. Lynn Davies went one better in Tokyo 1964, winning gold in the long jump.

Colin Jackson broke the world record for the 110 metres hurdles and won every gold medal there was to win apart from the one that really mattered – Olympic gold. Even so, he must rank as one of Wales's greatest ever athletes.

Tony Harris, the first Welshman to run a mile in under four minutes, and marathon runner Steve Jones are two others that deserve a mention. Dame Tanni Grey-Thompson, honoured for her services to disabled sport, is another world-class athlete who has done Wales proud.

On the snooker table, Tredegar-born Ray Reardon won six world championships in the 1970s.

When boxer Jim Driscoll (1880-1925) died more than 100,000 people are said to have stood along the route his funeral procession took to Cathays Cemetery in Cardiff. Driscoll, raised in abject poverty in the Newtown area of Cardiff, was dubbed 'Peerless' after his 'no decision' encounter with the American Abe Attell, who he completely out-boxed.

Driscoll, who was the first outright winner of a Lonsdale belt in the featherweight division, was unbeaten in 11 contests in the US.

Another fighter, Jimmy Wilde (1892-1969) had several nicknames and these included 'The Mighty Atom' and 'The Tylorstown Terror' but perhaps he was best known as 'The Ghost with the Hammer in his Hand'.

He was world flyweight champion from 1916-23, European flyweight champion from 1914-15 and 1916-1923, and British flyweight champion from 1916-1923.

Howard Winstone (1939-2000) won a gold medal at the Cardiff Empire & Commonwealth Games in 1958 and won a world featherweight title in 1968 when he beat Japan's Mitsunori Seki.

In more recent times, Newbridge's Joe Calzaghe held the WBO super middleweight title for more than 10 years and was undefeated in 46 fights before retiring in 2009.

▲ **Hero is hailed**
Crowds mob Jimmy Wilde at the end of his fight with Pal Moore in 1919

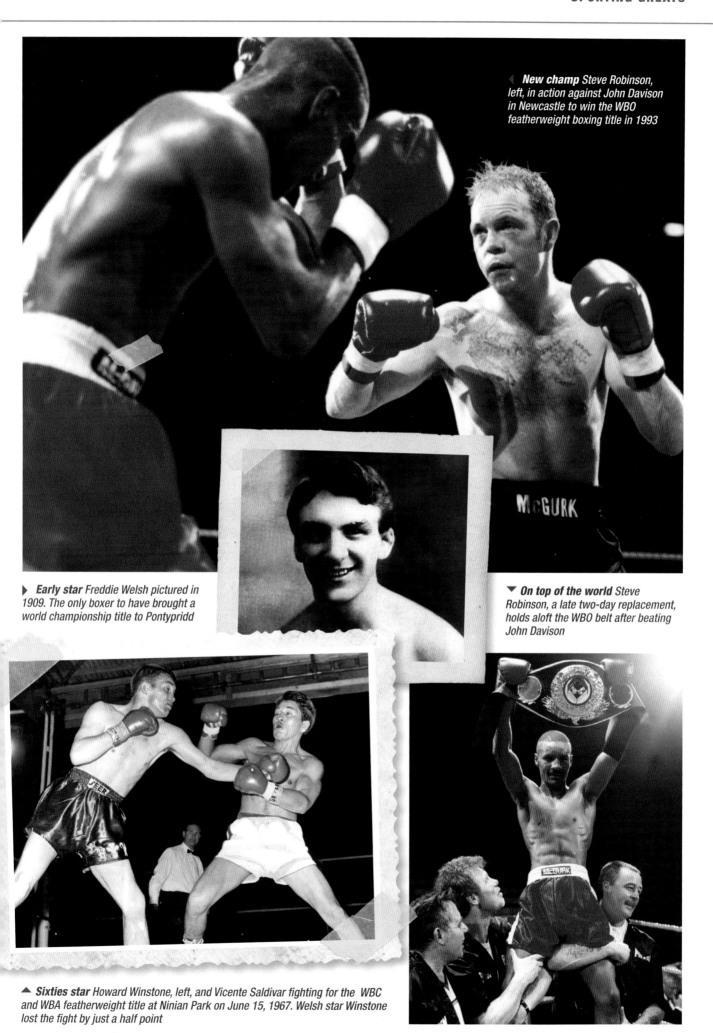

◀ **New champ** *Steve Robinson, left, in action against John Davison in Newcastle to win the WBO featherweight boxing title in 1993*

▶ **Early star** *Freddie Welsh pictured in 1909. The only boxer to have brought a world championship title to Pontypridd*

▼ **On top of the world** *Steve Robinson, a late two-day replacement, holds aloft the WBO belt after beating John Davison*

▲ **Sixties star** *Howard Winstone, left, and Vicente Saldivar fighting for the WBC and WBA featherweight title at Ninian Park on June 15, 1967. Welsh star Winstone lost the fight by just a half point*

▲ **Leap of glory**
Welsh long-
jumper Lynn
Davies, who won
gold at the Tokyo
Olympics in 1964
and was Britain's
flag-bearer in the
1968 Mexico City
games

▶ **For the high
jump** Welsh
Olympian Paulo
Radmilovic

Right on cue Ray Reardon in action during a tournament in January 1975

▲ *Snooker champ* Ray Reardon is pictured after winning the world professional snooker championship in April 1970. Presenting the trophy is Louise Mills, on behalf of the sponsors. Reardon, from Tredegar, won the Welsh amateur snooker title six times and, in 1964, the British amateur title

Inspiration Paralympian Tanni Grey-Thompson training on the roads near her Cardiff home in August 1990

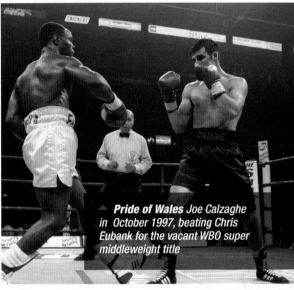

Pride of Wales Joe Calzaghe in October 1997, beating Chris Eubank for the vacant WBO super middleweight title

Going for glory Tony Harris wins the final of the 880-yard race at the Welsh AAA championships at Cardiff's Maindy Stadium in June 1967

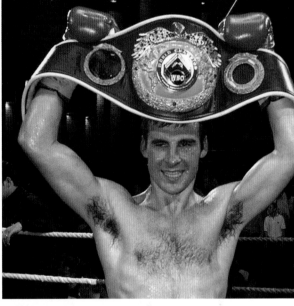

▲ *Still the best* Joe Calzaghe celebrates in August 2000 after retaining his WBO super middleweight title after victory over Omar Sheika at Wembley Conference Centre

◀ *Just denied* Colin Jackson in the 110m hurdles at the Sydney Olympics – he would be denied an Olympic gold to complete his superb career